FOREX

FOR BEGINNERS

*The Most Comprehensive Guide to Making
Money in the Forex Market
(2022 Crash Course for Newbies)*

Will Baxter

TABLE OF CONTENTS

INTRODUCTION

Congratulations and thank you for purchasing Forex for Beginners.

Did you know that the Forex market has a daily trading volume of $4 trillion? Why should you invest in the Forex market when so many other people are? To get started, all you need is a good internet connection and some basic knowledge, and this book will introduce you to the concepts of Forex trading that will help you get started and make money. If you want to invest in Forex, you don't even have to quit your day job. You can easily complete it in your spare time. Begin with a small amount and practise with a demo account.

After reading this book, you will have a thorough understanding of how everything works in this place. You will be introduced to the main players and will discover why the Forex market fascinates people all over the world. You will also learn more about trading plans and strategies, as well as how to create your own. The Forex market has been around for a long time, but it has recently gained popularity due to the availability of electronic trading, which has made the Forex market accessible to all. By the end of this book, you will be ready and prepared to make your first trade.

There are numerous books on this subject available; once again, thank you for selecting this one! Every effort has been made to ensure that it is as full of useful information as possible; please enjoy!

CHAPTER 1:

AN OVERVIEW OF THE FOREX MARKET

Before we get into the specifics of Forex trading, you should have a basic understanding of the Forex market, which we will cover in this chapter. Forex, or foreign exchange, is traded around the world by institutions, banks, and individual traders 24 hours a day, five days a week. Another feature of Forex is that there is no centralised marketplace. As a result, currencies are traded over-the-counter at any time, in any market that is open.

As a result, Forex is a global marketplace where different national currencies are exchanged for one another. Finance, commerce, and trade have a global reach in today's world, and as a result, Forex is frequently regarded as one of the most liquid and largest asset markets on the planet.

What exactly is the Forex Market?

The forex market is the location where all currency trading takes place. People may not realise it all the time, but currencies are important to everyone, regardless of where they live. This is primarily due to the fact that currency must be exchanged in order to conduct business or foreign trade. As a common civilian, you may recognise the significance of currency when travelling to a different country, such as Thailand. If you are from the United States, you will not be able to use US dollars in Thailand. You must first convert your US dollars into Thai baht before you can make purchases.

Zurich, Tokyo, New York, London, Hong Kong, Frankfurt, Sydney, and Paris are the major forex trading centres. As previously stated, the forex market is now open 24 hours a day.

The forex market opens as the trading day in the United States, Hong Kong, and Tokyo comes to an end. As a result, there is no specific time of day when you can be certain that the forex market will remain active. It is active at all times of the day and night, and the price quotes are constantly changing.

Different Types of Forex Markets

There are two main markets in the foreign exchange category, which are broadly classified as spot market and forward market, and we will learn more about them in detail.

Market on the Spot

Among the various types of Forex markets, this is where you will find the quickest transactions. In this type of market, both sellers and buyers will receive instant payment based on the current exchange rate. In fact, one-third of all transactions in the forex market are part of the spot market, and traders typically require 2-3 days to settle the transactions. As a result, traders can remain open to the volatility of the currency market. As a result, the price between the trade and the agreement can either fall or rise. A spot transaction occurs when a currency transaction is completed by the buyer and seller within two days of the date of the transaction. The rate at which the transaction is settled is referred to as the spot exchange rate.

The volume of such spot transactions in the forex market has skyrocketed. These transactions are typically carried out through banking system transfers, the cashing in of traveler's cheques, and the trading of currency notes. However, the banking system transfer is the most common, accounting for roughly 90% of total transactions.

These are carried out specifically by various banks.

Let's take a look at some of the main players in these types of transactions –

• **Commercial Banks** – The first participant, and the primary player in the spot market, are the commercial banks.

This is due to the fact that investment and commercial banks trade for both their customers and themselves. In fact, they aim to profit from currency movements, and thus the currencies put in by the bank account for the majority of transactions. If the transaction volume is large, the interbank transaction is also performed. However, if a small volume is involved, it may be done with the assistance of a broker.

• **Central Banks (CBs)** – The central bank of a country will intervene in the foreign exchange market to reduce fluctuations in that country's currency. Their goal is to ensure that the requirements of the national economy and the exchange rate of their currency are compatible. In fact, central banks may release some foreign currency into the market in order to prevent further depreciation of their own currency. By doing the opposite, they reduce the appreciation of their currency.

• **Brokers and Distributors** – Dealers make money by selling at high prices and buying at low prices. They are primarily involved in wholesale purchases and, in fact, perform the majority of interbank transactions. They may occasionally deal with central banks and corporations. They have a very thin spread, and the transaction costs are quite low. In terms of total transaction value in the forex market, wholesale transactions account for 90% of all transactions.

The Forward Market

In the case of a forward market contract, two entities or parties agree on a future date when the trade will take place at a specified quantity and price. Because no money is exchanged when the contract is signed, no security

13

deposit is required. The trade is usually made 90 days after the deal is signed.

You may be wondering whether or not this type of contracting has any advantages. There are some that you should be aware of – for starters, these types of contracts are commonly used in the context of speculation and hedging. There are market speculators who study everything, conduct extensive research, and then use that information to forecast whether the price will rise.

Then, if they believe there will be an increase, they buy currencies in the forward market rather than in cash. They would then simply wait, and if their prediction is correct and the price rises, they would sell the currencies at a higher price, bringing home a tidy profit.

But, along with these benefits, there are some drawbacks.

I've tried to be as succinct as possible in explaining them –

• There are no centralised rules for trading in the forward market, and it is highly illiquid due to the involvement of only two parties. There is always the risk of default, and thus there is counterparty risk.

The presence of a lot of generality and flexibility is the main problem or point of concern for traders in the first two problems I mentioned above. It's like negotiating a real estate contract with only two people present. These two people involved in the transaction are the only ones who get to decide the contract's terms based on what is convenient for them. If either of the two parties involved in the transaction declared bankruptcy, the other would suffer, which is known as counterparty risk, which is always present in the case of the forward market.

Another major consideration when trading in the forward market is the time span and its fluctuations. The greater the time span for which the contract is open, the greater the risk of large price movements. As a result, the counterpart risk in transactions continues to rise.

Forex Market Influencing Factors

The fluctuations and variations in currency exchange rates that you see are caused by a number of factors that affect the forex market directly or indirectly. They cause volatility, and if you want to trade in the forex market, you should be aware of these factors. Because Forex has evolved into a global marketplace, all macroeconomic events taking place around the world have a direct impact on currency exchange rates. With modernization, you don't have to focus solely on popular currencies, but for someone just starting out, popular currencies are a good option. Overall, it is safe to say that any new information or current events can quickly affect a country's economic health, and thus its exchange rates. Some of the most common factors to consider are listed below.

A country's political landscape

Any country's currency strength is heavily influenced by its economic performance and political situation. Foreign investors will be more interested in a country if political turmoil is less likely to occur in the coming days. This would imply that there would be an influx of foreign capital into that country, causing the domestic currency to appreciate. When a country's trade policy and financial situation are sound, they usually do not allow for any degree of currency uncertainty. However, in the case of countries experiencing political upheaval, exchange rates will frequently depreciate.

The economy will automatically flourish when the government is willing to take the necessary steps to improve everything in a country. As a result, investors seek out countries with stable governments because they know that such countries have a much better chance of growth and face fewer roadblocks. For example, when the news of Brexit became public, the GBP dropped in value in relation to the USD.

Inflation

This one, I believe, should come as no surprise, because if there is anything that has a direct impact on the currency, it is inflation. If a country's inflation rate is lower than that of the others, its currency value will follow the path of appreciation. When the rate of inflation is low, the prices of various goods and services rise slowly. Similarly, if any country's inflation rate is high, its currency will depreciate.

Now, for an investor, a currency with a lower rate of inflation would be appealing. For example, during a period of severe inflation in Zimbabwe, the Zimbabwe currency was aggressively devalued, and as a result, the

Zimbabwe currency does not hold an appealing position in the forex market.

Rates of Interest

The value of a currency and its exchange rates are heavily influenced by interest rates. Inflation, interest rates, and currency exchange rates are all interconnected. When interest rates rise, the value of a country's currency rises because lenders receive higher interest rates, implying a greater influx of foreign capital.

Debt of the Government

The Government debt refers to the national debt or public debt owed by the Central Government. Foreign capital is unlikely to enter a country with a large amount of government debt, which leads to an increase in inflation. If a country has government debt, foreign investors will sell the bonds on the open market. As a result, the value of the exchange rate will fall as a result.

Consider this: if someone who is already in a lot of debt comes to you and asks for money, would you be willing to give it to them? No, right? The same thing is going on here. Foreign investors examine a country's government debt over the last few years before deciding to part with their money.

Current Account of the Country

When a country makes a foreign investment, it creates a trade and earnings balance, both of which are reflected in the country's current account. All debt, imports, and exports are included in this category. The exchange rate depreciates when a country does not earn enough money from exports while also spending a lot of money on importing certain products. The exchange rate of the domestic currency varies according to the balance of payments.

Trade Conditions

In layman's terms, the terms of trade are simply the ratio of export prices to import prices. When the rate of increase in export prices exceeds the rate of increase in import prices in a country, trade conditions improve. As a direct result, the country's revenue increases. As a result, the value of that country's currency rises, and the currency is now in high demand. As a result, the exchange rate continues to rise.

If we look at it from the perspective of an investor, countries with lower imports and higher exports are more appealing.

Speculation

Among all other factors, this is not something that can be quantified. When there is speculation that a currency's rate will rise in the coming days, the rate of that currency rises. Investors from all over the world are expected to flock to the currency. But the catch is that you must identify this trend and exit it quickly because if you stay in it for too long and the trend ends, you will be the one who suffers.

So, these are some of the factors to be aware of if you intend to enter the forex market, as they influence the exchange rates of various currencies.

Stock Trading vs. Forex Trading

The first and most important reason why so many people prefer forex trading to stock trading is forex leverage. This, as well as several other points, will be covered in this section.

Leverage

When it comes to stock trading, margin account traders use 2:1 leverage. However, keep in mind that day traders can access leverage of up to 4:1 because they open and close their positions on the same day as long as their account balance is greater than $25,000.

Aside from that, the 4:1 leverage is only available if you meet a few other requirements. A margin account is not given to every investor, at least not right away, and in the case of stock trading, a margin account is required if you want to leverage.

But, when it comes to forex trading, a margin account is not required. Simply open a forex trading account if you want to use leverage in your trading. There are no prerequisites to meet. The amount of leverage varies from country to country. In the United States, the maximum leverage is 50:1, but in other countries, it can be leveraged up to 400:1.

As you may be aware, stock trading entails purchasing the shares of various companies. The price of these can vary greatly. It can range from tens of dollars to hundreds of dollars.

The price of these shares is determined by supply and demand.

However, in the world of Forex, things are very different. Yes, there is a chance that the exchange rate of a country's currency will fluctuate, but even so, you will have a large amount of currency at your disposal to trade with. This is why currency is such a liquid asset.

Trades that are paired

Currency quotations in trading are always done in pairs.

As a result, it simply means that you must consider both countries and their economies – the country whose currency you are trading against and the country whose currency you have chosen.

What you should be concerned about is also determined by the market.

If you have purchased Intel shares, your main concern is not what is happening to other companies and their shares, but whether or not the value of the stock you own will rise. However, if you look at the forex market scenario, you must be concerned about the economies of the countries whose currencies you are trading. Is one country more politically stable than the other? Does one of them have a higher GDP or a higher rate of job growth? These are the considerations you will need to make. As a result, when trading in the forex market, you must consider two financial entities rather than just one.

Forex trading is typically more sensitive to economic and political situations in other countries than stock trading.

The Impact of Trade Activity on Prices

The price sensitivity of the stock market to trade activity differs significantly from that of the Forex market. When 10,000 shares are purchased, the stock price may be affected, especially when small companies are involved. However, for larger companies or giants like Apple, this would barely scratch the surface.

On the contrary, even if there are a hundred million dollars in forex trades, the market price of the currency will not be affected in the least.

Access to the Market

In comparison to stock markets, currency markets have greater access. Well, in today's world, you can trade stocks all day (24 hours) and five days a week, but it won't be easy. However, because of the presence of several forex exchanges all over the world, you can easily do forex trading 24 hours a day, six days a week.

Finally, the regulations will give you far more freedom in the forex market than in the stock market. However, it is these regulations in the stock market that provide you with a level of protection that you will not find in the forex market.

CHAPTER 2:

FUNDAMENTAL AND TECHNICAL ANALYSIS IN FOREX.

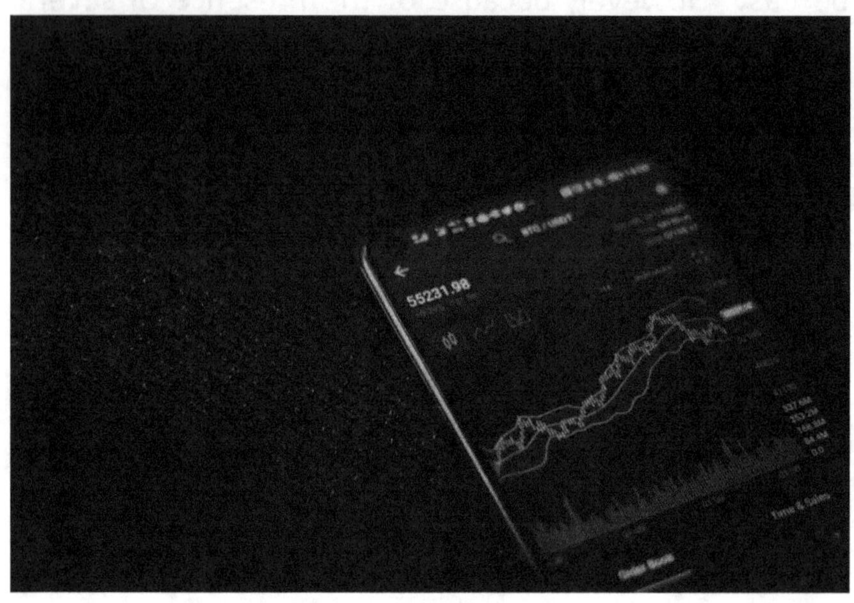

There are two types of market analysis that you should be aware of: technical analysis and fundamental analysis. These two options are not mutually exclusive, but if you ask any trader in the room, they will all fall into one of these two categories.

If we were to judge them objectively, I'd say they each have their own set of advantages and disadvantages. In this chapter, we will learn more about both of these types of analysis in depth.

Fundamental Examination

If you want to make accurate predictions about whether currency exchange rates will rise or fall, one method of evaluation is known as fundamental analysis. The basic idea behind fundamental analysis is that you must study and conduct research on various macroeconomic events in order to determine how they affect a specific currency. You must also keep an eye on social and political news, as well as any changes in monetary policy. This analysis must be performed for both currencies in the currency pair.

Let us say that you are working with a regional currency, for example, Euro – in that case, you have to analyse the entire regional economy along with the member states so that your evaluation of the financial status of the region turns out to be accurate.

In short, whenever there are some changes in the geopolitical or economic nature of a country, currency pairs react at once. This reaction can turn out to be even more drastic when the change occurs in a way that was not initially expected. That is why a fundamental analysis of the market is of utmost importance so that you can understand the changes that are going to happen in the exchange rates in the near future and in which way the market is going to move.

Tools

Let us now look at the various tools used in fundamental analysis in the forex market. First, there is historical data, followed by financial news from various types of media, and finally, there is the economic calendar.

The economic calendar will inform traders about the factors that can have an impact on a national currency, whether they are minor or major economic data. You will learn the exact time and date of these releases. Financial news broadcasts on various forms of media will inform you if there has been a major geopolitical event or any other economic change that you should be concerned about.

Then there are historical fundamental data, which will tell you whether the country has experienced a similar economic situation in the past and how the currency reacted in that situation at the time.

31

Indicators

In this section, we will go over some of the key indicators in fundamental analysis that will help you understand whether a potential change in the exchange rate is on the way or what the overall strength of the economy is right now. In fact, some of these indicators are so powerful and important that they may be able to predict whether the economy will turn down or up in the near future.

So, let us take a closer look at some of the most important indicators in the forex market –

• **Trade Balance** – As I explained in the first chapter, the trade balance is the difference between a country's total exports and total imports. This indicator has a direct impact on the country's currency and whether it is in demand or not. If the trade balance is positive and there is a surplus, it indicates that the country is doing well because imports are less than exports. If, on the other hand, the trade balance is negative and there is a deficit, it indicates that the country is underperforming and that the number of exports is less than the number of imports.

- **Employment Reports** – This refers to all types of job-related data, such as the total number of claimants or applicants for a specific service, the unemployment rate, and payroll levels, among other things.

- **Current Accounts** – The current accounts show all of a country's net cash transfers and balance of trade. If this figure shows a deficit, it means that the country is deeply in debt. However, if the amount is in surplus, it indicates that the country's total debts are less than its total foreign assets.

- **GDP – GDP** stands for Gross Domestic Product, and a country's currency is heavily based on this value.

If a country's GDP value rises, the economy is presumed to be in good and stable shape, and the

33

currency of the country will likely follow suit. This becomes even more pronounced if interest rates are expected to rise.

- **CPI –** This is an abbreviation for Consumer Price Index, and it is a key indicator of inflation. It operates at the consumer level and displays the prices of various products. Because the central banks of any country are highly focused on controlling the rate of inflation, CPI can influence the country's monetary policies.

When the rate of inflation rises, interest rates rise as well, and when consumer prices fall, interest rates fall as well.

- **PPI** – Prior to the production of a finished product, the amount paid by manufacturers for raw materials is denoted by PPI, or Producer Price Index. You're probably wondering how this affects a country's currency. Yes, because higher consumer inflation in the future is predicted by a higher PPI value, and vice versa.

• **National Credit Quality** – There are major agencies all over the world that give countries ratings based on whether they have defaulted on their loans or intend to repay them, and this will indicate the credit quality of that country. This would have a direct impact on the country's currency.

• **Commodity Prices** – Next, we have another important indicator that helps to identify disinflationary and inflationary cycles in both consuming and producing countries. Let's take crude oil as an example. If the price of crude oil falls, the first effect will be on transportation, and thus the costs of various goods will be influenced. In addition, the level of inflation would be reduced. However, if the price of crude oil rises, so will inflation.

Benefits and Drawbacks

Now that you have a basic understanding of what fundamental analysis is all about, let's look at some of its benefits and drawbacks.

35

The benefits are as follows:

• **Price Movement Explanation** – Price movements can happen very quickly, and as a beginner in the world of Forex, you may not always understand what is going on, which is where fundamental analysis comes in.

It will assist you in keeping up with economic reports and news, which are the primary drivers of price movements. When there is an unexpected economic change, the movements become even more dramatic.

• **Obtaining Valuation** – Every asset or financial instrument has a monetary value. So, as a trader, you will have to go through these values, and if you find that the current market price and the true value of an asset differ, it is your responsibility to figure out why. The fundamental analysis allows you to look at industrial production, consumer sentiment, inflation, interest rates, and other factors that can help you determine asset values.

• **Gain a Better Understanding of Global Markets –** Finally, fundamental analysis helps you gain a better understanding of global markets. If you know how to perform fundamental analysis, you can understand any country's economy in a single glance.

The drawbacks are as follows:

• **Information Overload –** The most obvious disadvantage that you will experience is that fundamental analysis can provide you with so much information that you feel overburdened. In fact, for a beginner, it can be quite overwhelming, and you may even miss out on important details in the midst of the chaos. As a result, the entire procedure becomes counterproductive.

• **Lack of Market Timing –** When it comes to exits and entries, fundamental analysis cannot really help you – yes, it will provide a broad overview, but not such minute technicalities, which are equally important.

37

And you should be aware that timing is the holy grail of trading, and you cannot afford to get it wrong. Thus, in order to know when to enter or exit a particular trade, you must use both technical and fundamental analysis.

- **Not Designed for the Short Term** – Another significant disadvantage is that, while you will receive economic fundamental data on a monthly basis, it will not be of much use to you in the short term. Because of the extreme volatility, there will be numerous spikes.

- **To a Great Extent Subjective** – Yes, there are concrete reasons for everything in fundamental analysis. However, an analyst who believes the price will move in a certain direction believes so for a variety of plausible reasons, and an analyst who believes the opposite will also provide several credible and concrete reasons.

- **Technical Evaluation**

In a nutshell, we use price movements in the past to perform technical analysis. In fact, you will often hear

38

analysts saying that this type of analysis involves less science and more art. Do you know why? It is because sometimes there are nuances occurring in between, mainly because the entire concept of technical analysis relies on predicting price movements based on past data. Thus, sometimes, conclusions might not be the same.

Price data is the first and foremost tool that is used in technical analysis. This is a very important consideration, and it doesn't matter what timeframe you have chosen for this. In fact, you will be provided with a framework through technical analysis that will help you to compare the present data to other historical occurrences of a similar type and study the present price action in detail.

Before we proceed, there are three very important things about technical analysis that you should know –

- Every technical analyst has the belief that the market participants can know everything that there is to know from the current trading price itself. Even if there is

39

some new piece of information, the trading price would quickly reflect it.

• The market always follows certain trends. And if you have a trained eye and notice price changes in a market, you will be able to spot these trends. And these trends are frequently very predictable.

• The market has always had a proclivity to repeat itself. As a result, trends are recursive. But I must warn you about something – even though history repeats itself, the trend might not appear in the exact same way as it did before.

There will be some resemblance, but there will also be some newness to it.

Tools

Now let us have a look at some of the common tools used in technical analysis –

40

- **Forex Volatility Tool** – This tool functions in a specific time period by providing the traders with a pip range.

The range of periods could be anything like a week or a day, and the range is the average in that time period. You will be able to set a proper target profit range when you know for certain what the volatility of your currency pair is.

- **Currency Correlation Tool** – The price movements of a currency pair can sometimes be related.

If two currencies move in the same direction, the correlation is said to be positive. Similarly, if the currency pair moves in the opposite direction, the correlation is said to be negative. When a trader follows a currency table, it becomes easier for them to notice and keep track of such relationships. Knowing these things will help you in better risk assessment and management of the same.

• **Price Action Analysis** – The balance between demand and supply in the market is identified through the price, and so it is a very important tool. In fact, there are traders who trade solely on the basis of price action analysis.

They identify the movements in price through the use of candlesticks.

• **Oscillators and Technical Indicators** – This is one of the most popular tools used by technical analysts.

There are several types of indicators included under this one, like Bollinger bands, RSI, MACD, Keltner channels, and so on.

Benefits and Drawbacks

Here are some of the advantages of technical analysis –

• **Can Be Done in Any Time Frame** – Whether you are trading in the long-term or short-term, technical analysis will be fruitful in all types of time frames.

• **Takes Market Timing Into Consideration** – Unlike fundamental analysis, you can detect your entry and exit from the market with the help of technical analysis. It will tell you when is the best time for executing a particular trade, and everything will be done in an efficient and methodical manner.

• **Helps You Analyze Trends** – Technical analysis uses different types of tools for detecting and studying different market trends. For example, support and resistance, swing highs and lows, moving averages, and so on.

• **Less Overwhelming** – Since there are a lot of things in fundamental analysis, it often gets tiring and overwhelming. But that is not the case with technical analysis because here, everything is a lot more simplified.

Price action is the primary variable everywhere in technical analysis, and so things are less complicated.

Now, let us look at some of the disadvantages –

• **Might Give You Mixed Signals –** One of the major drawbacks of technical analysis is that sometimes you might get mixed signals from the different indicators. For example, you might be getting a buy signal from one of the indicators, and at the same time, some other indicator might signal you to sell. This can get you confused and frustrated, and you might end up making the wrong decision.

• **Your Biases Might Influence It –** Technical analysts often get swayed by their biases. For example, if you have a bullish bias, you may overlook several signals pointing in the opposite direction.

The worst part is that you will be completely unaware that this is happening to you. Because there are so many technical tools available to you in today's world, you may end up overanalyzing the situation, which will only lead to confusion. You won't be able to take a distinct trading decision.

So, I know you might be wondering what to choose – technical analysis or fundamental analysis? Well, it depends entirely on you, but I would suggest you to use a mix of both. But remember that there is no right or wrong answer here. You simply have to use a particular approach and then see whether it works for you or not.

CHAPTER 3:

FUNDAMENTAL FOREX TRADING STRATEGIES YOU SHOULD BE AWARE OF

There are numerous trading strategies available in the world of Forex, but for traders who are just getting started, the most common question is which strategy to use.

In this chapter, we will answer that question by providing you with some common and simple strategies. These are the strategies you should always keep in your toolbox, and you will quickly realise that they have become a staple in your trading journey.

Once you've mastered these fundamental strategies, you'll feel more confident and prepared to move on to more advanced territory.

Breakout Investing

The first strategy we'll go over is something that everyone should learn no matter what. It is also very simple to understand, especially for someone who is just starting out. But, before we get into the specifics, I want you to understand what the term "breakout" means.

In layman's terms, a breakout occurs when price moves outside of resistance or support levels. When there is an increase in price that exceeds resistance levels, this is referred to as a bullish breakout. Then there are bearish breakout patterns, in which the price falls below the support levels.

But do you know why this strategy is regarded as so crucial?

The primary reason is that identifying a point of breakout also indicates that the market is entering a very volatile stage. And, if you're quick enough, you can even use this volatility to your advantage by spotting a trend early on and jumping on board.

Your goal should be to enter the market early and ride the trend until the volatility begins to subside. Your stop loss must then be placed at a point either below or above the breakout candle.

Crossover of Moving Averages

The average price will be constantly updated in this strategy, smoothing out the price data. This average's time period can be any length of time. It can be as much as 30 weeks or as little as 30 minutes – it all depends on what you choose. The best thing about this strategy is that it can be tailored to any time frame, making it suitable for both short-term and long-term traders.

One of the main reasons why traders prefer this strategy is that it aids in the identification of both resistance and support levels.

Traders who enjoy using technical analysis receive a signal when the price of an asset rises above a specific moving average.

Let us now discuss a simple price crossover – this is the most common trading strategy that employs moving averages. The simple price crossover occurs when the asset's price crosses either below or above the moving average. This indicates that the trend is about to shift.

Another common strategy employed by traders is the use of two moving averages. The first moving average is shorter, while the second is longer. When the shorter moving average crosses the longer moving average and rises above it, a buy signal is generated. This indicates that the price trend is rising, and you should sell the asset. This is also known as a golden cross, which is a popular term.

When the above-mentioned strategy generated a sell signal, it was a variation. When the shorter moving average crosses and falls below the longer moving average, this occurs. The indication is that the price trend is declining. This type of crossover is also known by a different name – death cross or dead cross.

Strategy Based on Trends

These strategies are ideal for those who are new to the forex market. Simply keep a close eye on the market for any changes or patterns. You must identify a trend and assume that the trend will continue in the same direction. There are a number of reasons why you should employ this strategy. To begin with, they are very easy to recognise. However, before acting on the trend, it must be confirmed. If you believe that trading on the trend entails identifying when the market is falling and buying, you are mistaken. It means you must identify the precise moment when the market appears to be on the verge of rising, and this is the time to buy.

Here are some indicators and how they can help you spot emerging trends.

Bollinger Bands (Bollinger Bands)

These are extremely useful because they help you identify market volatility. You can tell if the market is in an uptrend or a downtrend. If the bands are located at a point that is quite far away from the current trading price, the market is very volatile. Similarly, when the bands are very close to the current price, it means the opposite.

Both of these scenarios should be avoided, especially if you are a beginner. When the price reaches the upper band, you sell; when the price reaches the lower band, you buy.

Moving Averages (MA)

Moving averages are well-known for their ability to help you determine the direction of a trend. However, keep in mind that this indicator will not tell you whether the trend is ending or not, so relying solely on it would be a bad decision. When the current trading price falls below the moving average, you buy; when it reaches or exceeds the moving average, you sell.

Relative Strength Index (RSI)

This is a measure of how strong a market is relative to its peers. With the help of this indicator, you can determine whether an asset is overbought or underbought. When the RSI falls below 30%, an asset is said to be underbought, and when it rises above 70%, it is said to be overbought. If the price does not change but the RSI falls, you may be predicting a downtrend. So, before the downtrend begins, you should sell. However, relying solely on RSI is not an option. Other indicators must be used to confirm the signals.

Making Use of Trendlines

Another simple but effective strategy that you should learn is this one.

Simply draw a line connecting two price points (two highs or two lows) on the trading chart. If we assume that there is always some sort of trend in the forex market, then trendlines will help you determine which way the trend is moving – up or down. We do not always recognise certain economic effects or price movements on the charts with our naked eyes, and trendlines can help us do so.

However, if you've been noticing the price repeatedly bouncing off the same trendline, keep in mind that you're not alone – others are as well. True, this type of situation will help you get a few good entries one after the other, but keep in mind that the trendline will not last forever. So, before it fails, you must have your stop loss in place.

Traders who use the trend trading strategy employ a variety of tools, including stochastics, directional indices, volume measurements, RSI, and moving averages. All of these will assist you in identifying and evaluating trends.

Trade Carry

This is a specialised form of forex trading. When dealing with different currencies from different countries, there is often an interest rate difference, and if you can take advantage of this difference, that is what carry trade is all about. At the same time, I'd like to draw your attention to the fact that this type of forex trading can be extremely risky.

However, it is also quite popular.

The basic working principle of this strategy is that the currencies are purchased one day and then held overnight.

The trader profits from the interbank interest rate in this manner.

The catch is that you must choose a country that will provide you with a lower rate of interest and purchase currency from them in order to fund your next purchase, which will be a currency with a higher rate of interest than the previous one. Isn't it amazing? The difference between these two rates is what you will profit from. The amount of leverage you use will determine how much profit you make, and keep in mind that it can be substantial!

This is one of the most popular strategies in the world of forex trading, but as I previously stated, it can also be quite risky, and the main reason for this is that there can be overcrowding due to excessive leverage.

However, two popular trading pairs for this strategy are the New Zealand dollar/Japanese Yen and the Australian dollar/Japanese Yen.

These pairs are commonly used because the interest rate spread in these pairs is quite wide and can be used to your advantage.

Trading based on momentum

Momentum trading is yet another popular strategy used by forex traders. Traders use recent price trends to buy and then sell currencies.

Assume a trader is using the momentum forex trading strategy and notices that the price of an asset has begun to move in a specific direction; they place a bet that the direction of movement will remain unchanged.

Certain aspects of trading, such as the rate of a price change or trading volume, are used to define momentum. In fact, did you know that when it comes to high volumes, there is always that one stock in the market every day that can move up by as much as 30%? This is heavily dependent on certain announcements and news releases, which you must not miss.

So, the main idea behind momentum trading is that when traders see a strong movement in price in one direction, they believe the price will continue to move in that direction for a set period of time. Similarly, they like to believe that if a movement has weakened, it means that the trend is likely to die down. Traders in momentum trading typically employ visual analysis tools such as candlestick charts and oscillators.

Trading in the Range

Let us now discuss another popular, yet very simple, forex trading strategy – range trading. This strategy is based on the assumption that currency prices will remain within a fixed price range when considered over a limited time period. However, this type of trading strategy should be used only if the economy is predictable and, more importantly, stable. You must also be certain that no unexpected news events are on the horizon that could jeopardise your plans.

Traders who use the range trading strategy buy and sell currencies frequently, and they do so at resistance and support highs and lows. In fact, they could do it multiple times in a single trading session.

When it comes to determining an exit and entry point, range traders and trend traders use tools that are similar.

Stochastics, commodity channel index, and relative strength index are examples of these.

Making use of the Purchasing Power Parity Indicator

If you're looking for profitable trading strategies that are also simple to implement as a beginner, using Purchasing Power Parity levels and comparing exchange rates to them is a good place to start.

If you're wondering what the Purchasing Power Parity indicator is, it's a tool that helps you determine the rate at which the average prices of various services and goods can be equalised. So, if a currency has been trading at a price lower than the PPP, it is said to be undervalued.

59

Similarly, if a currency's exchange rate is greater than the PPP, it is overvalued.

But don't misunderstand me. Just because you've decided to use the PPP indicator for forex trading doesn't mean the market will always behave the same way. However, if you look at the major currencies, you will notice that their trading ranges remain within a 20% range, give or take.

This strategy is popular among beginners due to its simplicity, but there is one thing to keep in mind: the strategy works best when considering trades with a longer time horizon. However, if you consider a shorter time span, such as a daily basis, you will notice that the exchange rates vary greatly and continue to diverge from the PPP levels by large numbers. And the balance will not be restored anytime soon – it may take weeks.

So, now that you've learned about all of the major beginner strategies, the key to selecting the right strategy for yourself is to select the appropriate level of risk management, good money, and leverage. If you do not adhere to all of the fundamental principles, no matter how good your strategy is, you will suffer massive losses.

If you want to become a professional in forex trading, you must hone your skills and develop sound trading strategies. You will also need a trading plan, which you will learn about in the latter part of this book.

Once all of this is in place, you can gradually progress to more complex strategies. Maintain realistic expectations while having fun with what you're doing.

CHAPTER 4:

HOW TO DEVELOP THE RIGHT TRADING MINDSET

Developing the right trading mindset is critical to success, but many people fail to recognise this. When it comes to trading, your greatest enemy will be your fear of making mistakes or losing money, and that fear can be overcome by honing your skills and working on your mindset. Trading psychology is a topic that researchers all over the world are interested in. It deals with the fact that you need to change your personality so that you can keep your emotions in check and not let them mess with your head while trading.

Being a successful trader entails more than just conducting extensive market statistics analysis or devising better trading strategies; it also entails developing the proper trading mindset. However, most new traders believe that if they can only find the perfect strategy, they will be able to make a lot of money. But that's not how it works – it's not that simple. If all you needed was a well-thought-out strategy, we'd all be billionaires by now.

There are people who have good strategies but continue to lose large sums of money every day.

And there are some traders who have consistently done well in the forex market because they have developed the psychologically correct mindset, which is what separates winners from losers.

The world of forex trading necessitates the development of certain psychological characteristics, attitudes, and beliefs that will assist you in making more money and succeeding in forex trading.

What exactly is a trading mindset?

Before I give you some tips on how to improve your trading mindset, you should first understand what a trading mindset is. You must understand that the market is devoid of any morality or emotions. So, if you want to continue trading in the long run and make some substantial profits from it, you must also develop the right mindset for it, which can happen once you learn how to observe the market without becoming emotionally attached to it.

All of your actions are ultimately determined by the mindset you maintain. Depending on your mindset, you can either make huge profits or suffer huge losses. Even if you do suffer a loss, having the right mindset will keep you from succumbing to panic and allow you to make rational decisions. You cannot afford to make any decisions based on your emotions, which is what trading psychology is all about.

65

A disciplined trader will never let anything get in the way of their trading decisions. However, becoming a disciplined trader is not easy, and it does not happen overnight. You must put in an equal amount of effort, willpower, and time to become the disciplined trader required to make successful trades.

Why Is It Important for You to Have a Positive Attitude?

As you are aware, there are no emotions associated with the market; the only emotions at work are those of the market participants. This is also why the various trendfollowing techniques and charting patterns work so well. They are primarily based on dominant market psychology and human behaviour.

I'm not sure if you've heard this famous phrase, but there's a saying that within 90 days, 90 percent of trading funds or 90 percent of traders will be lost. That means that successful market traders account for only 10% of the market, so what distinguishes them?

The answer is a positive mindset, which you will learn how to develop in this chapter.

Some traders believe that the market and everything else is rigged against them – this type of negative mindset stifles their growth. If your thoughts and decisions are clouded by such opinions, you will never be able to analyse the market objectively. It's important to remember that the market doesn't care whether you win a lot of money or lose everything – it's completely unbiased in that regard.

Thus, if you observe or speak with any successful trader, or read their interviews, you will notice one thing in common with all of them – selfconfidence. They have faith in their abilities and in themselves in general – having a positive mindset and outlook is essential. This belief should not be shaken no matter how many trades you lose.

Traders who consistently lose, on the other hand, frequently have this looming self-doubt bothering their minds. They believe that bad luck follows them all the time, that they are cursed, or that they are in some other way cursed. And, over time, this erroneous belief becomes a self-fulfilling prophecy. When you are unsure of your own decisions or abilities, you will be hesitant to take action or initiate trades when you should have, and you will miss out on profit-making opportunities as a result. When it comes to trading, it is pointless to be overly fearful of everything, and you must understand this from the start.

Yes, even the best market analysis cannot always explain price movements, but you must acknowledge and respect this and not blame it on the market being out to get you because there is no such thing. Here Are Some Mindset-Grooming Tips

To excel at trading, you must maintain a relaxed and calm mindset. You must also implement the appropriate risk management strategies, which you will learn about in the following chapter. For the time being, you must understand that even if you lose a trade or two, it is not the end of the world. Even today's most successful traders have lost trades, and it happens all the time. If you can maintain a winning percentage of 50% and your reward-to-risk ratio is high enough, you will be able to take home large sums of money. Instead of focusing on winning all trades, you should concentrate on one trade at a time. If you fail, learn from your error and try again. If you win, don't think of yourself as someone who will never make a mistake. Continue to be humble and to trade.

Also, when trading, you must learn not to take things personally. A bad trade is exactly what it appears to be: a bad trade. It has nothing to do with personal feelings. The market may not perform in the same manner every day, so you must simply apply everything you have learned and maintain faith in the market analysis that you are performing.

So, here are some pointers to help you develop a trader's mindset and win more trades.

Continue to Learn

Remember that in the world of trading, there is always something new to learn. Newer strategies, modes of analysis, and so on are available. You must remain a student for the rest of your life. In fact, one of the most important factors that distinguishes a successful trader from an unsuccessful one is continuing to educate yourself about the trading world and forex markets. This book will help you lay the groundwork for your trading career, and if you follow everything I've mentioned here, you'll have a comprehensive understanding of how to continue trading.

Education in forex trading will help you understand certain market reactions and, as a result, price movements. You will be able to make more accurate predictions this way. In the world of forex trading, there are countless concepts to learn. There is literally no end to the list, but what you must do is determine which of these concepts or strategies works best for you, and then continue to hone your skills and that strategy over time.

There is one thing you can do to make learning a habit: choose a trading book and promise yourself that you will read it for at least an hour before going to bed or at any other time of day when you think you will have time. Many well-known and successful traders encourage

71

beginners to engage in this practise. You can also try out some of the online trading courses that are now available.

Never Allow Losses to Control Your Decisions.

When new traders lose trades, they have a tendency to let their emotions cloud their judgement. In fact, some traders believe that they must always close in a win, and as a result, they continue to trade and make bad decisions even when the market requires them to do the opposite. So, do you see how emotions caused by losses can jeopardise your trading career?

You must learn to limit your losses. If you notice that one of your trades is not performing as expected, don't wait. Get out of it as soon as possible and try to limit your losses. You must move on to better trades rather than continuing to lose money on the same trade.

Understand how to Adjust to the Market

The market conditions will not be consistent at all times. The market may be performing well today, but in a few weeks, months, or days, it may completely reverse its current position and begin moving in the opposite direction. You must be equally adaptable in order to accommodate these changes in your strategy.

Maintain a neutral point of view before analysing the market.

If your analysis indicates that it is time to change your trading strategy, you must do so. Don't let your emotions or preconceived notions cloud your market analysis. Never be afraid to put your research to the test.

Don't Overburden Yourself

There will be times when everything becomes jumbled, the market is erratic, and your original strategy no longer applies to the current situation. You must maintain an objective perspective regardless of what is going on around you. This is what will discipline you as a trader. If the market appears to be too chaotic to handle and you believe you are unprepared, don't worry too much and wait for the dust to settle. When you notice a signal that you recognise, you can seize the opportunity. Whatever trading strategy or setup you use, it must have become second nature to you by now. If you intend to start a new business, practise it in market conditions that you are familiar with. Only use that trading setup in crisis situations after you've mastered it.

Be Consistent

Finally, I'd like to emphasise that no one became a successful trader overnight. To become an expert at something, takes time, patience, and experience. Just because you have suffered a few setbacks does not imply that you will give up and leave. Take it as a learning opportunity, and let your mistakes teach you something.

Keep a journal in which you will record all of your trades, such as your entry and exit points and why you chose to enter that trade in the first place. You can also jot down any additional remarks you want your future self to remember.

By keeping a trading journal, you will be able to identify a plethora of trading patterns throughout your journey. It will assist you in honing your abilities.

So, now that you've finished the chapter, I'd like to remind you that if you're serious about becoming a successful trader, you can't sit on your couch and procrastinate. You must get up and make an actual effort. Every trade, as we all know, comes with its own set of risks, and risk management is an equally important part of being a successful trader, which brings us to our next chapter.

CHAPTER 5:

MANAGING MONEY AND RISKS TO AVOID LOSSES

In this chapter, I'll give you a crash course in how to minimise your losses and maximise your profits in forex trading by using the right money and risk management strategies. Many beginners believe that if they can predict the direction of price movement in the forex market, they have won the trade; however, this is only one side of the coin. Risk management is the other side of the coin. Trading in the forex market always carries a high level of risk, and if you do not take steps to mitigate that risk, you will lose money one way or another.

Traders, particularly newcomers, have a bad habit of ignoring this aspect of trading; however, this is not a wise thing to do. However, if you want to be successful in trading, there are a few risk management rules that you must follow, and we will go over those rules in detail in this chapter.

Before we get into the rules, I'd like to introduce you to the various types of risk that you'll encounter in the forex market.

- **Interest Rate Risk** – Another risk posed by volatility is interest rate risk. Market volatility is what causes

77

abrupt changes in interest rates. When the economy as a whole is considered, there is a change in the amount of investment and spending, which affects foreign exchange rates.

• **Currency Risk** – Finally, there is currency risk, which occurs when the prices of currencies fluctuate, causing the currencies to become less or more expensive when purchasing foreign assets.

• **Leverage Risk** – This applies to traders who trade on margin because they run the risk of having their losses greatly magnified. Because the value of the forex trade, in this case, is much greater than the initial outlay, novice traders frequently forget how much money they are putting at risk.

• **Risk of Liquidity** – This is when you want to avoid a loss but are unable to do so because you are unable to sell or buy the currency as quickly as you need to. Yes, I know I said at the beginning of this book that one of the benefits of forex trading is its high liquidity, but there may be times when there is illiquidity. This is mostly due to the implementation of certain government policies that abruptly change the playing field for everyone.

- **Use capital that you can afford to lose.**

The first and most important tip for managing your money and limiting your risk is to only trade with money you can afford to lose. It's really quite simple. Do you have to deposit a certain amount of money into your trading account? As a result, this sum should not be greater than what you can afford.

To make the process easier, evaluate your monthly expenses. Then, after giving it some thought, set a specific value that you are willing to lose in a month. You must keep in mind that if you have already reached this level, you must immediately cease trading. The main point of this tip is that you should not be putting money at risk that could completely turn your life upside down if

79

you lose it. As a result, a good rule of thumb is to avoid trading with money that you need for necessities. This includes the money you need each month to pay your mortgage, rent, commuting expenses, food, and other bills, among other things.

Remember that, while trading can make you a lot of money, it is not a guaranteed way to make money. As a result, you will make a lot of mistakes and lose money before you learn to trade successfully. As a result, don't lose any money that you can't afford to lose.

• **Don't try to time the market.**

Now, let us move on to the next most important aspect of forex trading: you must resist the urge to chase the market. When someone is new to forex trading, they do not understand the risks that come with chasing every trading opportunity. Some of them may not have a high enough chance of winning, and chasing such a trade setup will almost certainly result in a large loss. New traders are frequently so excited about their new trading account and being in the forex market that they overlook other critical factors. They even place multiple trades within an hour because they believe one of them will profit them, but things don't work that way. When someone engages in this type of behaviour, it is more akin to gambling than trading.

You must remember that there is nothing owed to you by the market. To be a successful trader, you must have a lot of patience, which you will realise as time goes on. For example, if you do not find enough solid trading opportunities on a given day, you must take a step back and wait for your entry the following day. Chasing the market will get you nowhere. No matter how much profit you have made, remember that a single losing trade can wipe out all of your gains.

• Learn to quantify the amount of money at stake in each trade.

I already stated in the first point that you should not trade with money that you require for day-to-day living expenses. So, once you've determined how much money you're going to put into your trades, it's time to determine how much you're risking in each trade. But why do you require this? Calculating the risking value, on the other hand, will assist you in determining the stop loss.

Quantifying your risk is simple, and there are two methods from which to choose –

• A Predetermined Percentage – The first method is the most common, in which you set a fixed percentage of your trading account balance to risk in each trade. So, if your trading account has a balance of $10,000 and you have decided to quantify your risks at 2%, then every trade you make will involve a risk of $200. So, what is the

82

benefit of using this method? It ensures that if you lose a trade, your entire account balance is not lost. Furthermore, because you have set it at 2%, the more trading capital you have, the more you can risk in any trade. However, there is a drawback to this method. If someone has suffered a string of losses, their account balance will have plummeted significantly, and the amount of money they have left or are willing to risk is very small. As a result, recouping your losses will take time.

- **A Fixed Sum –** Another school of thought holds that your risk limit per trade should be set at a fixed amount rather than a fixed percentage. For example, a trader may decide to risk $500 in each trade after depositing $10,000 in their trading account. The rule is not difficult to remember or follow. The advantage is that you know exactly how much money is at stake with each trade. So, if you decide to make a total of five trades per day, the maximum amount of money you can lose is $2,500 and no more. The disadvantage of this system is that you risk $500 in every trade, regardless of how much money you have in your trading account. At the same time, if your trading account balance has increased significantly as a result of several consecutive wins, you will not be risking much and will thus miss out on higher returns simply because you thought of risking only $500 in each trade. On the other hand, if you have lost a maximum portion of your money and only have $2,000 in your account, risking $500 in every trade means risking a significant portion of your total trading account.

• Create an Effective Trading Strategy

You can only make your forex trading experience much easier if you have a well-designed trading plan. It will serve as a guide to assist you in making trading decisions. In fact, when the market becomes volatile, it can be difficult to make the right decisions at the right time, but a good trading plan can make it easier and encourage discipline. If your trading plan is properly constructed, it should answer the questions of when what, how much, and why you are trading.

Every trading strategy is unique. The main idea behind creating trading plans is that they should be personal to you, with your own ideas and personal touch. It will not help you to simply replicate someone else's trading strategy. The main reason for this is that the person you are copying may not share your goals. Because their ideas and attitudes may differ from yours, their trading strategy will not work for you. Another significant difference between your trading strategy and that of others is the amount of money you are willing to risk in trading – it may not be the same as the other person's.

Finally, I'd like to emphasise the importance of keeping a trading journal or diary – this will allow you to keep track of all the trades you make and strategies you employ. You should also keep track of your emotional state during each trade. In the following chapter, we will go over how to create a trading plan in depth.

• Minimize Your Losses

A general rule of thumb in all forms of trading – whether forex trading or any other type of trading – is to limit your losses.

In simpler terms, if you notice that one of your trades is not performing well and that things have not turned out the way you expected, the losses from your trade will continue to accumulate.

In that case, you must close the trade as soon as possible.

Similarly, if your business is doing well, you should keep it going, but only to a certain point. You must set a stop loss and refrain from being overly greedy – you never know when everything will change. Keep an eye on market conditions so that you can exit the trade at the right time and profit handsomely.

This rule is frequently broken by new traders. When they start losing money in a trade, they believe that keeping it open will allow them to wait for the course to eventually run in the opposite direction. Similarly, they may exit profitable trades too soon because they are afraid of losing money.

Greed and fear are two of the most dangerous emotions to allow to fester in the trading world. If you want to advance in your trading career, you must let go of these emotions.

You learned in the previous steps that you must set a fixed amount of money that you are willing to risk in each trade. Once that is completed, the next step is to determine how much profit you want to make in the next trade. This will be the take profit level for each trade.

Your profit goal will be heavily influenced by your trading profile and the strategies you employ. Most importantly, your risk tolerance will determine your profit-taking threshold.

Assume you've set your risk-to-reward ratio to 1:1; this means that if your acceptable amount of loss is $200, your profit target in that trade should also be $200. However, if someone has a risk-to-reward ratio of, say, 1:3, they would have a target profit of $600 with the same acceptable loss of $200.

In forex trading, the general rule of thumb is that your risk-to-reward ratio should be greater than 1:1. Do you understand why? This is due to the fact that even if you lose two trades in a row and then win two trades in a row, you will have a net profit; however, if the ratio was 1:1, your net profit would have been $0.

• Make use of Limits and Stops

Volatility, as you may have guessed, is a common occurrence in the forex market. As a result, even before you open a new position during a trade, you must have your exit points prepared.

There are various types of limits and stops that can help you with this –

• **Guaranteed Stops –** These stops will ensure that you exit the trade at the price that you specify. The risk of slippage can be avoided in this case.

• **Normal Stops –** Then there are normal stops, whose main function is to find their own position when the market begins to move in the opposite direction. However, slippage protection is not guaranteed here.

- **Trailing Stops** – The nature of these stops is such that they closely follow positive price movements, and whenever a move works against you, the trailing stop will exit your position in the trade.

- **Limit Orders** – The main goal here is to set a takeprofit level and then adhere to it. Your position will be closed once the profit has reached that level.

- **Exercise Caution When Using Leverage**

One of the most common mistakes in trading is using too much leverage, especially among beginners. You must understand that, while leverage allows you to trade more, it is essentially a two-edged sword. It is true that leverage will allow you to increase your profits tenfold, but it is also true that if things do not go as planned, the same leverage will cause you to lose ten times more money.

Trading on leverage is the most appealing aspect of forex trading because it allows you to keep increasing the volume of your trading account. But, at its core, this is not the way to trade.

The first thing to remember as a trader is that you must safeguard your capital. When you open a position, always consider the downside of the trade, and before you consider your potential profit, consider your potential loss. Several factors should be considered when determining the appropriate amount of leverage, such as the size of your trading account, the stop-loss distance, and the risk-per-trade that you have determined.

• Keep Currency Correlations in Mind

We all know that in the forex market, currencies are bought and sold in pairs, and they are priced in the same way. So, in order to be a successful trader in the forex market, you must first understand the relationship between these currencies.

You will be able to build a better Forex portfolio as a result, and your overall risks will be reduced. You will continue to have complete control over everything.

But what exactly does correlation imply? It entails examining the changes in one currency caused by a change in the price of the other currency in the pair. If the currencies have a positive correlation, they will move in the same direction. Similarly, if there is a negative correlation between them, they will move in the opposite direction.

• Manage Your Emotions

Beginners in trading frequently allow their emotions to interfere with their trading decisions, which is something you cannot afford to do.

92

The high level of volatility in the forex market will elicit strong emotions in you, but you must not allow yourself to become overwhelmed. Emotions such as doubt, temptation, greed, fear, and anxiety will prevent you from seeing things objectively and will cause you to think from your heart. Allowing your emotions to take over will, however, have a negative impact on the outcome of your trade.

So, if you're just getting started, all of the money and risk management tips in this chapter should help you find the right path. Once you've made your trading decisions, it's critical that you stick to them no matter what. And, like anything else in life, becoming a better trader necessitates a lot of practise. If you are a complete novice, you can begin with a demo account.

With a demo account, you can test your strategies and make mistakes without fear of losing money. Demo accounts allow you to trade with virtual funds rather than risking your real money and losing it. As a result, you will gradually gain a better understanding of how the forex market works. You can also use your demo account to back-test your strategies and trading plan, determining where there is room for improvement.

It's okay to make mistakes, but it's also important to learn from them and promise yourself not to repeat them. If you experience losses, learn to accept responsibility for them. Don't play the blame game and blame the market for your loss – you need to understand that it is only you who determines what happens to the money in your trading account.

CHAPTER 6:

HOW DO YOU MAKE A TRADING STRATEGY?

What we mean by a trading plan is nothing more than a guide or a map to assist the investor in making proper decisions regarding this trade and to highlight to him what the risks are, what the profit points are, and to assist him in drawing out a plan so that his business runs smoothly. A proper trading plan should ideally tell an investor what his objectives should be in order to achieve that goal, what risks he may face, and how much time he will need to get there. Technically, an ideal trading plan should also identify the most profitable entry and exit points for the investor, as well as the proper position sizing rules.

The plan should ideally include position sizing rules, risk management techniques, how he will find the trade, and how he will execute it in return. The plan should also specify the appropriate time and conditions under which the investor can buy or sell securities, as well as the types of securities that must be purchased in the first place. The type of securities to be dealt with, as well as the nature and position of their management, are all important details that should be included in the trading plan.

A trading plan, which is essentially a management guide, should also guide you in developing a proper trading system. It is ultimately a well-drafted trading plan that will assist the investor in working in the market with minimal problems, and thus it must be well researched and well-drafted, and it should also ideally provide the investor with adequate space for making any changes or adjustments later so that any kind of emergency can be met at short notice. Every investor is expected to have some personal preferences, objectives, and a distinct approach to their work in the market. As a result, it is the trading plan that informs us about their distinct approach and style, which distinguishes them from other investors.

A trading plan is an essential part of any financial transaction that is highly recommended by every expert to their next in line, as any serious investment is bound to be backed by a well-made and well-thought-out trading plan. Everyone who is new to this field should understand from the start that it is critical to develop a detailed trading plan before embarking on an investing plan. Those who have been in this business for a while will already know that your trading plan should ideally include a summary of all the key points regarding each step you intend to take so that you have a clear picture of what you are getting yourself into. Having a clear idea of the strategies you want to employ will keep you prepared for everything that is to come. Overall, your trading plan will make the entire process of forex trading much easier for you, making it a much more convenient initiative to take.

What is the Purpose of a Trading Strategy?

Having a trading point is critical because it allows you to transition from theory to experience. It is ultimately the trading plan that helps you actualize it, from reading and learning about the entire trading and investment plan to actually practising it in the real market. Doing anything without proper knowledge will only result in a slew of issues and impending disasters. However, having prior knowledge of it makes it easier. No amount of reading about trading and marketing will ever provide you with the necessary expertise. It's similar to learning to drive, and obtaining a licence isn't enough. You will never gain confidence unless you drive that car on a busy road by yourself. Similarly, unless you make a plan and start acting on it, you will not gain enough experience to make a difference. Only by sticking to a plan will you learn about your own limitations and strengths, allowing you to take more informed decisions.

How to Make a Profitable Trading Strategy

We have already discussed what a trading plan is and why it is critical to have a detailed trading plan before beginning forex trading. Now that we've established the importance of having a plan, let's talk about how to

99

actually create one in real life. We understand that it can be intimidating at times, but don't worry. We've got you covered. I've listed some simple, easy-to-understand steps for creating a trading list below to help you understand the process so you can improve your skills.

- **Recognize your abilities -** This is primarily for your benefit. It is up to you to decide whether you want to trade or not. Then ask yourself what kind of trading you want to do next. What are the risks you are willing to take, what do you believe your strengths are, and how much do you believe you can handle? You are now ready to move forward with your planning after you have obtained these answers from yourself.

- **Self-preparation -** After you've decided what you want and what you expect, it's critical to prepare yourself both physically and mentally for what's ahead. It is highly recommended that you do not neglect any physical needs, such as proper food and rest, prior to the day of trading, as you will need all of your strength. Simultaneously, if anything is bothering you mentally, it is best to deal with it ahead of time so that you have nothing to distract you on that day.

- **Set your goals -** It is critical for both beginners and experienced traders to have a clear picture of their risk/reward ratio. You should have a clear idea of what your objectives are. If you begin with extremely ambitious goals, you may find it extremely difficult to achieve those goals for the first time. As a result, you may become dissatisfied with your actions in the future. However, this is not the ideal situation. So, in the beginning, it's always a good idea to get your head around the actual practical picture and set yourself goals that you won't have too much trouble achieving. Once you know what you want, it will be much easier to work toward achieving it.

- **Set an upper limit for your risk level -** You must understand that no matter how emotionally invested you

101

are in a particular trade, if you can estimate that it is going up above the risk limits you can handle, you must reform your strategies or, in extreme cases, change your plans entirely. You simply cannot allow yourself to exceed a certain level of risk. Set a limit for yourself. Anywhere between 1% and 5% is acceptable. If the trade you've taken up remains within this limit, it means you'll be able to rearrange your strategies in the event of an emergency. Anything above that indicates that you should reconsider the trade before proceeding.

• **Do your homework thoroughly -** Before you begin anything, you must conduct a thorough background check on everything related to your project.

Learn whether the currencies you want are rising or falling in value, and conduct thorough research on both your domestic and international markets. Don't forget to double-check all of the data pertaining to economic policies. This is one of the most important parts of your trading process because a large portion of your trading policies will be based on market analysis and data, so you must get these right.

- **Carefully plan your trade -** You must choose a method that works best for you in order to keep track of your trade journals. Once you've decided how to keep track of your trade, you'll need to label the minor and major resistance and support levels. After that, create a convenient alert for each of your entry and exit points.

- **Establish rules for entry and exit -** Because both entry and exit points are critical in any trade, you can't prioritise one over the other. Plan them ahead so that no problems arise later. You need to analyse your profit targets and breakeven points for setting the rules of your \sentry and exit points. What this will do is also help you by giving you an additional option B, in case things go wrong with your option A.

• **Properly maintain your records** - Once you've gathered all of your data, your job is to keep it organised and up to date. Make a list of your long-term and short-term strategies. This will be your guidebook for \handling any situation.

• **Analyze your performance -** Your trading plan will be your best critic because it will give you a clear picture of all your past and present trading actions, allowing you to see how your future trades should be. It will make you learn from your mistakes and help you increase your future profit margins.

CONCLUSION

Thank you for reading Forex for Beginners all the way to the end; we hope it was informative and provided you with all of the tools you need to achieve your goals, whatever they may be.

Every day, a large number of people begin trading in the forex market. It is not difficult to get started. You only need to do some research and take the first step. And if you've arrived at this point in the book, you're ready to take the first step. With the rise of the internet, forex trading is no longer a difficult task. In fact, it has become more convenient and accessible. Forex trading has grown significantly in recent years, and now is the time to put your skills to use and make money.

But I strongly advise you to first devise a strategy. Don't get too involved right away. Make a plan and stick to it regardless of what happens. Slow and steady wins the race in trading. As you continue to place trades, you will learn more about the market. These lessons will help you succeed in the long run. Make the most of a demo account because it will allow you to practise trading in an environment that mimics the market while remaining risk-free, which means you will not lose any money here.